I'M NOT AS FAST AS A CHEETAH

Written by: Jeff Rout

Illustrated by: Arlene Ouellette

"I'm Not as Fast as a Cheetah" Soft cover book

ISBN: 978-0-9867593-9-0

Copyright © 2020 by Domino Effect Publishing
All rights reserved.
No part of this book may be used or reproduced in any manner whatsoever without explicit written permission by the publisher except in the case of brief quotations embodied in critical articles and reviews and where otherwise permitted by Canadian and/or US Copyright Law.

Written by: Jeff Rout
Ilustrations Pencilled and Inked by: Arlene Ouellette
Vector Art, Colouration, and Layout by: Jeff Rout

Categories:

1 - JUVENILE NONFICTION / Philosophy
2 - JUVENILE NONFICTION / Social Topics / Values & Virtues
3 - JUVENILE NONFICTION / Social Topics / Self-Esteem & Self-Reliance

I'M NOT AS FAST AS A CHEETAH

Written by: Jeff Rout

Illustrated by: Arlene Ouellette

I'm not as fast as a cheetah.

I can run.

I'm faster than some people, and I'm slower than others.

But I'm not as fast as a cheetah.

Being the fastest isn't that important.

Some people do bad things with their speed.

That's not good.

Some people do good things with their speed.

That is good.

We can't all be the fastest, but we can all be good.

You don't need to be fast at all to be good.

Being good matters more than being fast.

I'm not as strong as a moose.

I have strength.

I'm stronger than some people, and I'm weaker than others.

But I'm not as strong as a moose.

Being the strongest isn't that important.

Some people do bad things with their strength.

That's not good.

Some people do good things with their strength.

That is good.

We can't all be the strongest, but we can all be good.

You don't need to be strong at all to be good.

Being good matters more than being strong.

I'm not as smart as an owl.

I have intelligence. I'm smarter than some people, and I'm less smart than others.

But I'm not as smart as an owl.

Being the smartest isn't that important.

Some people do bad things with their intelligence.

That's not good.

Some people do good things with their intelligence.

That is good.

We can't all be the smartest, but we can all be good.

You don't need to be smart at all to be good.

Being good matters more than being smart.

I may not be the fastest, strongest, or smartest.

But I can use what I have to do good.

And that's good enough.

www.ingramcontent.com/pod-product-compliance
Lightning Source LLC
Chambersburg PA
CBHW061818290426
44110CB00026B/2906